OTHER EDITIONS OF *THE MESSAGE*:
The New Testament, Psalms and Proverbs
The Old Testament Wisdom Books
(Job, Psalms, Proverbs, Ecclesiastes, Song of Songs)
Job
Psalms
Proverbs
The Message Promise Book
Sayings of Jesus
Messages for the Heart
(60-minute audio cassette)

HIS UNFOLDING GRACE

DAILY MEDITATIONS FROM

NOT A DAY GOES BY WITHOUT

HIS
UNFOLDING
GRACE

EUGENE H. PETERSON

NAVPRESS

BRINGING TRUTH TO LIFE

NavPress Publishing Group

P.O. Box 35001, Colorado Springs, Colorado 80935

ISBN 1-57683-107-8

Published in association with the literary agency of
Alive Communications, Inc., 1465 Kelly Johnson Blvd., Suite 320,
Colorado Springs, CO 80920.

Printed in the United States of America

1 2 3 4 5 6 7 8 9 10 11 12 13 14 15 / 05 04 03 02 01 00 99 98

CONTENTS

INTRODUCTION

PERHAPS the best way to figure out how to live our days is to frame them one by one in the very practical wisdom of God's Word. After all, it is in the Bible, God's "Message" to us, that we discover just how much he understands our joys, our sorrows, our triumphs, and our temptations. He is "God with us" on our pilgrimage.

The book you hold in your hands is a kind of daily dialogue between you and God. God's part of the dialogue comes from his Word, presented here as a biblical mosaic of various passages on a specific topic. So the dialogue begins with God's voice. Reading directly from Scripture, you listen to God speak. After mulling over what God says, letting God's Word soak into the present details of your life just as it is, it is time for you to enter the dialogue: Write down what you're feeling, thinking, seeing. Your journal becomes a record of your God-accompanied journey.

Eventually, as you look over your journal entries, you'll see threads running through the pages—white threads of joy, black threads of suffering, and a broad spectrum of colors in between, woven into the kind of beautiful but demanding complexity that makes up a human life. You will also detect the golden threads of God that unify and bring meaning to the tapestry.

As you look for direction from the God who is with you in your journey, you do well to stay in close conversation with him. God very much wants to both speak and listen to you. So set forth on your daily journey with God at the center of your life, and you will discover the dynamic nature of his unfolding grace.

MAKE THE MOST OF EVERY CHANCE YOU GET

IF YOU'VE GOTTEN ANYTHING at all out of following Christ, if his love has made any difference in your life, if being in a community of the Spirit means anything to you, if you have a heart, if you care—then do me a favor: Agree with each other, love each other, be deep-spirited friends. Don't push your way to the front, don't sweet-talk your way to the top. Put yourself aside, and help others get ahead. ~

"You've observed how godless rulers throw their weight around," Jesus said, "and when people get a little power how quickly it goes to their heads. It's not going to be that way with you. Whoever wants to be great must become a servant. Whoever wants to be first among you must be your slave. That is what the Son of Man has done: He came to serve, not to be served—and then to give away his life in exchange for many who are held hostage." ~

I have a word for you who brashly announce, "Today—at the latest, tomorrow—we're off to such and such a city for the year. We're going to start a business and make a lot of money." You don't know the first thing about tomorrow. You're nothing but a wisp of fog, catching a brief bit of sun before disappearing. Instead, make it a habit to say, "If the Master wills it and we're still alive, we'll do this or that." As it is, you are full of your grandiose selves. All such vaunting self-importance is evil. ~

So watch your step. Use your head. Make the most of every chance you get. These are desperate times! ~ Stay calm. Mind your own business. Do your own job. ~ Mortals make elaborate plans, but God has the last word.

൯ ൬

[Phil. 2:1-3; Mk. 10:42-45; Jas. 4:13-16; Eph. 5:15-16; 1 Thes. 4:11; Pr. 16:1]

How can you know whether the things you want to accomplish are good or bad, right or wrong?

DON'T LASH OUT

GOD IS sheer mercy and grace; not easily angered, he's rich in love. He doesn't endlessly nag and scold, nor hold grudges forever. He doesn't treat us as our sins deserve, nor pay us back in full for our wrongs. ~ God is good to one and all; everything he does is suffused with grace. ~

Slowness to anger makes for deep understanding; a quick-tempered person stockpiles stupidity. ~ Complain if you must, but don't lash out. Keep your mouth shut, and let your heart do the talking. ~ A word out of your mouth may seem of no account, but it can accomplish nearly anything—or destroy it! It only takes a spark, remember, to set off a forest fire. ~

Let angry people endure the backlash of their own anger. If you try to make it better, you'll only make it worse. ~ Don't hang out with angry people. Don't keep company with hotheads. Bad temper is contagious—don't get infected. ~

Jesus said, "You're familiar with the command to the ancients, 'Do not murder.' I'm telling you that anyone who is so much as angry with a brother or sister is guilty of murder. . . . The simple moral fact is that words kill. ~

"When someone gives you a hard time, respond with the energies of prayer, for then you are working out of your true selves, your God-created selves. This is what God does. He gives his best—the sun to warm and the rain to nourish—to everyone, regardless: the good and bad, the nice and nasty." ~

Post this at all the intersections, dear friends: Lead with your ears, follow up with your tongue, and let anger straggle along in the rear. God's righteousness doesn't grow from human anger.

ᏊᎧ ᎧᏊ

[Ps. 103:8-10; Ps. 145:9; Pr. 14:29; Ps. 4:4; Jas. 3:5; Pr. 19:19; Pr. 22:24-25; Mt. 5:21-22; Mt. 5:45; Jas. 1:19-20]

What are the best ways of dealing with anger when you feel it welling up inside of you?

CHANGED FROM THE INSIDE OUT

HERE'S WHAT I WANT you to do, God helping you: Take your everyday, ordinary life—your sleeping, eating, going-to-work, and walking-around life—and place it before God as an offering. Embracing what God does for you is the best thing you can do for him. Don't become so well-adjusted to your culture that you fit into it without even thinking. Instead, fix your attention on God. You'll be changed from the inside out. Readily recognize what he wants from you, and quickly respond to it. Unlike the culture around you, always dragging you down to its level of immaturity, God brings the best out of you, develops well-formed maturity in you. ~

Your new life is not like your old life. Your old birth came from mortal sperm; your new birth comes from God's living Word. Just think: a life conceived by God himself! ~ In kindness he takes us firmly by the hand and leads us into a radical life change. ~

So don't try to get out of anything prematurely. Let it do its work so you become mature and well-developed, not deficient in any way. ~ You see farmers do this all the time, waiting for their valuable crops to mature, patiently letting the rain do its slow but sure work. Be patient like that. Stay steady and strong. The Master could arrive at any time. ~

God wants the combination of his steady, constant calling and warm, personal counsel in Scripture to come to characterize *us*, keeping us alert for whatever he will do next. May our dependably steady and warmly personal God develop maturity in you so that you get along with each other as well as Jesus gets along with us all.

ও৹ ৹ও

[Rom. 12:1-2; 1 Pet. 1:23; Rom. 2:4; Jas. 1:4; Jas. 5:7-8; Rom. 15:4-5]

Since it's virtually impossible for a feeling, thinking person to stay exactly the same, change is inevitable in everyone's life. What kinds of changes have you observed within yourself, and in what ways do you want to change in the future?

He'll Carry Your Load

GOD COMES ALONGSIDE US when we go through hard times, and before you know it, he brings us alongside someone else who is going through hard times so that we can be there for that person just as God was there for us. We have plenty of hard times that come from following the Messiah, but no more so than the good times of his healing comfort—we get a full measure of that, too. ~

We've been surrounded and battered by troubles, but we're not demoralized; we're not sure what to do, but we know that God knows what to do; we've been spiritually terrorized, but God hasn't left our side; we've been thrown down, but we haven't broken. ~ We're not giving up. How could we! Even though on the outside it often looks like things are falling apart on us, on the inside, where God is making new life, not a day goes by without his unfolding grace. ~ Distress that drives us to God does that. It turns us around. It gets us back in the way of salvation. We never regret that kind of pain. ~

God's a safe-house for the battered, a sanctuary during bad times. ~ God is a safe place to hide, ready to help when we need him. We stand fearless at the cliff-edge of doom, courageous in seastorm and earthquake, before the rush and roar of oceans, the tremors that shift mountains. ~

Pile your troubles on God's shoulders—he'll carry your load, he'll help you out. ~ Jesus said, "Are you tired? Worn out? Burned out on religion? Come to me. Get away with me and you'll recover your life. I'll show you how to take a real rest."

[2 Cor. 1:4-5; 2 Cor. 4:8-9; 2 Cor. 4:16; 2 Cor. 7:10; Ps. 9:9; Ps. 46:1-3; Ps. 55:22; Mt. 11:28]

In what ways do you need to be comforted? In what ways can you comfort others?

UNLIKE THE CULTURE AROUND YOU

DON'T BECOME so well-adjusted to your culture that you fit into it without even thinking. Instead, fix your attention on God. You'll be changed from the inside out. Readily recognize what he wants from you, and quickly respond to it. Unlike the culture around you, always dragging you down to its level of immaturity, God brings the best out of you, develops well-formed maturity in you. ~

Don't become partners with those who reject God. How can you make a partnership out of right and wrong? That's not partnership; that's war. Is light best friends with dark? Does Christ go strolling with the Devil? Do trust and mistrust hold hands? Who would think of setting up pagan idols in God's holy Temple? But that is exactly what we are, each of us a temple in whom God lives. ~

So watch your step, friends. Make sure there's no evil unbelief lying around that will trip you up and throw you off course, diverting you from the living God. For as long as it's still God's Today, keep each other on your toes so sin doesn't slow down your reflexes. ~

God tested us thoroughly to make sure we were qualified to be trusted with this Message. Be assured that when we speak to you we're not after crowd approval—only God approval. Since we've been put through that battery of tests, you're guaranteed that both we and the Message are free of error, mixed motives, or hidden agendas. ~ Anyone who gets so progressive in his thinking that he walks out on the teaching of Christ, walks out on God. But whoever stays with the teaching, stays faithful to both the Father and the Son.

એન ઉજ

[Rom. 12:2; 2 Cor. 6:14-16; Heb. 3:12-13; 1 Thes. 2:3-4; 2 Jn. 9-11]

DAY 5

What in your life do you feel so strongly about that you would never be willing to compromise?

CULTIVATE GOD-CONFIDENCE

FAR BETTER to take refuge in God than trust in people. ~ Blessed are you who give yourselves over to God, turn your back on the world's "sure thing," ignore what the world worships. ~ When we trust in him, we're free to say whatever needs to be said, bold to go wherever we need to go. ~ God doesn't want us to be shy with his gifts, but bold and loving and sensible. ~

Saving is all God's idea, and all his work. All we do is trust him enough to let him do it. It's God's gift from start to finish! We don't play the major role. If we did, we'd probably go around bragging that we'd done the whole thing! ~ There's no such thing as self-rescue, pulling yourself up by your bootstraps. ~

Don't be so naive and self-confident. You're not exempt. You could fall flat on your face as easily as anyone else. Forget about self-confidence; it's useless. Cultivate God-confidence. ~

Test yourselves to make sure you are solid in the faith. Don't drift along taking everything for granted. Give yourselves regular checkups. You need firsthand evidence, not mere hearsay, that Jesus Christ is in you. Test it out. If you fail the test, do something about it. ~

Let's not just talk about love. Let's practice real love. This is the only way we'll know we're living truly, living in God's reality. It's also the way to shut down debilitating self-criticism, even when there is something to it. For God is greater than our worried hearts and knows more about us than we do ourselves. ~ But you need to stick it out, staying with God's plan so you'll be there for the promised completion.

⌒⌒⌒

[Ps. 118:8; Ps. 40:4; Eph. 3:12; 2 Tim. 1:7; Eph. 2:8-9; Ps. 49:7; 1 Cor. 10:12; 2 Cor. 13:5; 1 Jn. 3:18-20; Heb. 10:36]

Are you more confident about yourself, others, or God? In what way should this be modified?

LESS IS MORE AND MORE IS LESS

LESS IS MORE and more is less. ~ A pretentious, showy life is an empty life; a plain and simple life is a full life. ~ "If you puff yourself up, you'll get the wind knocked out of you. But if you're content to simply be yourself, your life will count for plenty." ~

Actually, I don't have a sense of needing anything personally. I've learned by now to be quite content whatever my circumstances. I'm just as happy with little as with much, with much as with little. I've found the recipe for being happy whether full or hungry, hands full or hands empty. Whatever I have, wherever I am, I can make it through anything in the One who makes me who I am. ~ A devout life does bring wealth, but it's the rich simplicity of being yourself before God. Since we entered the world penniless and will leave it penniless, if we have bread on the table and shoes on our feet, that's enough. ~

Don't be obsessed with getting more material things. Be relaxed with what you have. ~ As long as you grab for what makes you feel good or makes you look important, are you really much different than a babe at the breast, content only when everything's going your way? ~

So be content with who you are, and don't put on airs. God's strong hand is on you. He'll promote you at the right time. Live carefree before God; he is most careful with you. ~ Be content with obscurity, like Christ.

⌦ ⌫

[Ps. 37:16; Pr. 13:7; Mt. 23:12; Phil. 4:11-13; 1 Tim. 6:6-8; Heb. 13:5; 1 Cor. 3:3; 1 Pet. 5:6-7; Col. 3:4]

Imagine two different scenarios in which you have both a lot more and a lot less than you have now (not just materially but in terms of popularity, friendships, talents, etc.). In which of these three contexts—the two scenarios plus the way things are now—do you think you'd be most content? How does God factor into the whole matter of contentment?

GOD IS A SAFE PLACE

HELP, GOD—the bottom has fallen out of my life! Hear my cry for help! ~ You're my last chance, my only hope for life! Oh listen, please listen. I've never been this low. ~

I've tried everything and nothing helps. I'm at the end of my rope. Is there no one who can do anything for me? ~ I waited and waited and waited for God. At last he looked. Finally he listened. He lifted me out of the ditch, pulled me from deep mud. He stood me up on a solid rock to make sure I wouldn't slip. He taught me how to sing the latest God-song, a praise-song to our God. More and more people are seeing this: they enter the mystery, abandoning themselves to God. ~ God is a safe place to hide, ready to help when we need him. We stand fearless at the cliff-edge of doom. ~

God remembered us when we were down. ~ It was so bad we didn't think we were going to make it. We felt like we'd been sent to death row, that it was all over for us. As it turned out, it was the best thing that could have happened. Instead of trusting in our own strength or wits to get out of it, we were forced to trust God totally— not a bad idea since he's the God who raises the dead! And he did it, rescued us from certain doom. *And* he'll do it again, rescuing us as many times as we need rescuing. ~

When life gets really difficult, don't jump to the conclusion that God isn't on the job. Instead, be glad that you are in the very thick of what Christ experienced. This is a spiritual refining process, with glory just around the corner. ~ "You're blessed when you're at the end of your rope. With less of you there is more of God and his rule."

෴෴

[Ps. 130:1; Ps. 142:5-6; Rom. 7:24; Ps. 40:1-3; Ps. 46:1-2; Ps. 136:23; 2 Cor. 1:8-10; 1 Pet. 4:12-13; Mt. 5:3]

In what ways has God touched your life when you were feeling down?

THE LIFE-MAPS OF GOD

THE LIFE-MAPS of God are right, showing the way to joy. The directions of God are plain and easy on the eyes. ~ God is fair and just. He corrects the misdirected, sends them in the right direction. ~ Every God-direction is road-tested. Everyone who runs toward him makes it. ~ We plan the way we want to live, but only God makes us able to live it. ~

If you find life difficult because you're doing what God said, take it in stride. Trust him. He knows what he's doing, and he'll keep on doing it. ~ Trust God from the bottom of your heart. Don't try to figure out everything on your own. Listen for God's voice in everything you do, everywhere you go. He's the one who will keep you on track. Don't assume that you know it all. Run to God! Run from evil! ~

For sound advice is a beacon, good teaching is a light, moral discipline is a life path. ~ Wise men and women are always learning, always listening for fresh insights. ~ Without good direction, people lose their way. The more wise counsel you follow, the better your chances. ~

So watch your step. Use your head. Make the most of every chance you get. These are desperate times! Don't live carelessly, unthinkingly. Make sure you understand what the Master wants. ~ Figure out what will please Christ, and then do it. ~ Be energetic in your life of salvation, reverent and sensitive before God. That energy is *God's* energy, an energy deep within you, God himself willing and working at what will give him the most pleasure. ~ You need to stick it out, staying with God's plan so you'll be there for the promised completion.

∽◉∾

[Ps. 19:8; Ps. 25:8; Ps. 18:30; Pr. 16:9; 1 Pet. 4:19; Pr. 3:5-7; Pr. 6:23; Pr. 18:15; Pr. 11:14; Eph. 5:15-17; Eph. 5:10; Phil. 2:12-13; Heb. 10:36]

How do you usually determine what direction to take in the big decisions of your life?

His Unfolding Grace

IF YOUR HEART IS BROKEN, you'll find God right there. If you're kicked in the gut, he'll help you catch your breath. ~ We've been surrounded and battered by troubles, but we're not demoralized; we're not sure what to do, but we know that God knows what to do; we've been spiritually terrorized, but God hasn't left our side; we've been thrown down, but we haven't broken. ~ Even though on the outside it often looks like things are falling apart on us, on the inside, where God is making new life, not a day goes by without his unfolding grace. ~

Those of us who are strong and able in the faith need to step in and lend a hand to those who falter, and not just do what is most convenient for us. Strength is for service, not status. ~ Gently encourage the stragglers, and reach out for the exhausted, pulling them to their feet. Be patient with each person, attentive to individual needs. ~ Let's see how inventive we can be in encouraging love and helping out. ~

If you give encouraging guidance, be careful that you don't get bossy; if you're put in charge, don't manipulate; if you're called to give aid to people in distress, keep your eyes open and be quick to respond; if you work with the disadvantaged, don't let yourself get irritated with them or depressed by them. ~ Never walk away from someone who deserves help; your hand is *God's* hand for that person. ~ God comes alongside us when we go through hard times, and before you know it, he brings us alongside someone else who is going through hard times so that we can be there for that person just as God was there for us.

∽◦ ◦∾

[Ps. 34:18; 2 Cor. 4:8-9; 2 Cor. 4:16; Rom. 15:1; 1 Thes. 5:14; Heb. 10:24; Rom. 12:8; Pr. 3:27; 2 Cor. 1:3-4]

What have been the most encouraging times in your life? What can you do to encourage someone else?

OUR HANDLE ON WHAT
WE CAN'T SEE

IT'S IMPOSSIBLE TO PLEASE God apart from faith. And why? Because anyone who wants to approach God must believe both that he exists *and* that he cares enough to respond to those who seek him. ~ The fundamental fact of existence is that this trust in God, this faith, is the firm foundation under everything that makes life worth living. It's our handle on what we can't see. ~

Do you think you'll get anywhere in this if you learn all the right words but never do anything? Does merely talking about faith indicate that a person really has it? For instance, you come upon an old friend dressed in rags and half-starved and say, "Good morning, friend! Be clothed in Christ! Be filled with the Holy Spirit!" and walk off without providing so much as a coat or a cup of soup—where does that get you? Isn't it obvious that God-talk without God-acts is outrageous nonsense? ~

So don't lose a minute in building on what you've been given, complementing your basic faith with good character, spiritual understanding, alert discipline, passionate patience, reverent wonder, warm friendliness, and generous love, each dimension fitting into and developing the others. ~ It's what we trust in but don't yet see that keeps us going. ~ For in Christ, neither our most conscientious religion nor disregard of religion amounts to anything. What matters is something far more interior: faith expressed in love.

꙳ ꙳

[Heb. 11:6; Heb. 11:1; Jas. 2:14-17; 2 Pet. 1:5-7; 2 Cor. 5:7; Gal. 5:6]

What does faith look like in your life?

DAY 11

TO GIVE AND FORGIVE

LIVE CREATIVELY, friends. If someone falls into sin, forgivingly restore him, saving your critical comments for yourself. *You* might be needing forgiveness before the day's out. ~ When you were stuck in your old sin-dead life, you were incapable of responding to God. God brought you alive—right along with Christ! Think of it! All sins forgiven. ~ As far as sunrise is from sunset, God has separated us from our sins. ~ God's readiness to give and forgive is now public. Salvation's available for everyone! ~

Be gentle with one another, sensitive. Forgive one another as quickly and thoroughly as God in Christ forgave you. ~ Don't laugh when your enemy falls. Don't crow over his collapse. ~ If you see your enemy hungry, go buy him lunch; if he's thirsty, bring him a drink. Your generosity will surprise him with goodness, and God will look after you. ~

Jesus said, "Love your enemies. Let them bring out the best in you, not the worst. When someone gives you a hard time, respond with the energies of prayer." ~ "In prayer there is a connection between what God does and what you do. You can't get forgiveness from God, for instance, without also forgiving others. If you refuse to do your part, you cut yourself off from God's part." ~ "If you forgive someone's sins, they're gone for good. If you don't forgive sins, what are you going to do with them?" ~

But sin doesn't have a chance in competition with the aggressive forgiveness we call *grace*. When it's sin versus grace, grace wins hands down. ~ Smart people know how to hold their tongue. Their grandeur is to forgive and forget.

✂ ✂

[Gal. 6:1; Col. 2:13; Ps. 103:12; Titus 2:11; Eph. 4:32; Pr. 24:17; Pr. 25:21-22; Mt. 5:44; Mt. 6:14-15; Jn. 20:23; Rom. 5:20; Pr. 19:11]

Think of times in your life when you have received forgiveness and given forgiveness.

FREE TO PURSUE WHAT GOD WANTS

SINCE WE'RE FREE in the freedom of God, can we do anything that comes to mind? Hardly. You know well enough from your own experience that there are some acts of so-called freedom that destroy freedom. Offer yourselves to sin, for instance, and it's your last free act. But offer yourselves to the ways of God and the freedom never quits. ~

Jesus said, "If you stick with this, living out what I tell you, you are my disciples for sure. Then you will experience for yourselves the truth, and the truth will free you." ~ "If the Son sets you free, you are free through and through." ~

Can't you see the central issue in all this? It is not what you and I do. It is what *God* is doing, and he is creating something totally new, a free life! ~ It is absolutely clear that God has called you to a free life. Just make sure that you don't use this freedom as an excuse to do whatever you want to do and destroy your freedom. Rather, use your freedom to serve one another in love. That's how freedom grows. For everything we know about God's Word is summed up in a single sentence: Love others as you love yourself. That's an act of true freedom. If you bite and ravage each other, watch out—in no time at all you will be annihilating each other, and where will your precious freedom be then? ~

Christ has set us free to live a free life. So take your stand! Never again let anyone put a harness of slavery on you. ~ Then you'll be able to live out your days free to pursue what God wants instead of being tyrannized by what you want.

෴

[Rom. 6:15-16; Jn. 8:31-32; Jn. 8:36; Gal. 6:15; Gal. 5:13-15; Gal. 5:1; 1 Pet. 4:2]

DAY 13

What do you consider to be genuine freedom?

DAY 13

You're Always Young in God's Presence

AY AND NIGHT I'll stick with God. I've got a good thing going and I'm not letting go. I'm happy from the inside out—and from the outside in, I'm firmly formed. ~ I'm just as happy with little as with much, with much as with little. I've found the recipe for being happy whether full or hungry, hands full or hands empty. ~

A pretentious, showy life is an empty life; a plain and simple life is a full life. ~ You're addicted to thrills? What an empty life! The pursuit of pleasure is never satisfied. ~ Watch out for the Esau syndrome: trading away God's lifelong gift in order to satisfy a short-term appetite. ~

We pray that you'll have the strength to stick it out over the long haul—not the grim strength of gritting your teeth but the glory-strength God gives. It is strength that endures the unendurable and spills over into joy. ~ "You're blessed when the tears flow freely. Joy comes with the morning." ~ "When a woman gives birth, she has a hard time, there's no getting around it. But when the baby is born, there is joy in the birth. This new life in the world wipes out memory of the pain. The sadness you have right now is similar to that pain, but the coming joy is also similar." ~

Laugh with your friends when they're happy; share tears when they're down. ~ God wraps you in goodness—beauty eternal. He renews your youth—you're always young in his presence. ~ Celebrate God all day, every day. I mean, *revel* in him!

☙ ❧

[Ps. 16:8-9; Phil. 4:12; Pr. 13:7; Pr. 21:17; Heb. 12:16; Col. 1:11; Lk. 6:21; Jn. 16:21-22; Rom. 12:15; Ps. 103:5; Phil. 4:4]

How can you "Celebrate God all day, every day"?

LOVE FROM THE CENTER OF WHO YOU ARE

LOVE FROM THE CENTER of who you are. Don't fake it. ~ Love never gives up. Love cares more for others than for self. Love doesn't want what it doesn't have.

Love doesn't strut, doesn't have a swelled head, doesn't force itself on others, isn't always "me first," doesn't fly off the handle, doesn't keep score of the sins of others, doesn't revel when others grovel, takes pleasure in the flowering of truth, puts up with anything, trusts God always, always looks for the best, never looks back, but keeps going to the end. Love never dies. ~

Let's not just talk about love. Let's practice real love. ~ Don't love the world's ways. Don't love the world's goods. Love of the world squeezes out love for the Father. ~

Loving God includes loving people. You've got to love both. ~ Jesus said, "'Love the Lord your God with all your passion and prayer and intelligence.' This is the most important, the first on any list. But there is a second to set alongside it: 'Love others as well as you love yourself.'" ~

With both feet planted firmly on love, you'll be able to take in with all Christians the extravagant dimensions of Christ's love. Reach out and experience the breadth! Test its length! Plumb the depths! Rise to the heights! Live full lives, full in the fullness of God. ~

Learn to love appropriately. You need to use your head and test your feelings so that your love is sincere and intelligent, not sentimental gush. ~ Anyone who claims to be intimate with God ought to live the same kind of life Jesus lived.

∾ ∾

[Rom. 12:9; 1 Cor. 13:4-8; 1 Jn. 3:18; 1 Jn. 2:15; 1 Jn. 4:21; Mt. 22:37-39; 1 Tim. 1:5; Eph. 3:17-19; Phil. 1:9-10; 1 Jn. 2:6]

DAY 15

How can you love "appropriately" with a love that is "sincere and intelligent, not sentimental gush"?

LOSING THE CAPACITY FOR TRUTH

WATCH THE WAY you talk. Let nothing foul or dirty come out of your mouth. Say only what helps, each word a gift. ~ Don't talk out of both sides of your mouth. Avoid careless banter, white lies, and gossip. ~ A gadabout gossip can't be trusted with a secret, but someone of integrity won't violate a confidence. ~ Though some tongues just love the taste of gossip, Christians have better uses for language than that. Don't talk dirty or silly. That kind of talk doesn't fit our style. Thanksgiving is our dialect. ~

God's angry displeasure erupts as acts of human mistrust and wrongdoing and lying accumulate, as people try to put a shroud over truth. ~ The person who tells lies gets caught. The person who spreads rumors is ruined. ~ These liars have lied so well and for so long that they've lost their capacity for truth. ~

How long will you lust after lies? How long will you live crazed by illusion? ~ Tell your neighbor the truth. In Christ's body we're all connected to each other, after all. When you lie to others, you end up lying to yourself. ~ If we claim that we experience a shared life with God and continue to stumble around in the dark, we're obviously lying through our teeth—we're not *living* what we claim. ~

Truth lasts. Lies are here today, gone tomorrow. ~ God keeps his word even when the whole world is lying through its teeth.

☙ ❧

[Eph. 4:29; Pr. 4:24; Pr. 11:13; Eph. 5:4; Rom. 1:18; Pr. 19:9; 1 Tim. 4:2; Ps. 4:2; Eph. 4:25; 1 Jn. 1:6; Pr. 12:19; Rom. 3:4]

In what situations do you sometimes say things that are not true or pure?

LIFE IS NOT DEFINED BY WHAT YOU HAVE

DON'T WEAR YOURSELF OUT trying to get rich. Restrain your-self! Riches disappear in the blink of an eye—wealth sprouts wings and flies off into the wild blue yonder. ~ Lust for money brings trouble and nothing but trouble. Going down that path, some lose their footing in the faith completely and live to regret it bitterly ever after. ~

Jesus said, "Do you have any idea how difficult it is for people who 'have it all' to enter God's kingdom?" ~ "Don't hoard treasure down here where it gets eaten by moths and corroded by rust or—worse!—stolen by burglars. Stockpile treasure in heaven, where it's safe from moth and rust and burglars. It's obvious, isn't it? The place where your treasure is, is the place you will most want to be, and end up being." ~

A life devoted to *things* is a dead life, a stump; a God-shaped life is a flourishing tree. ~ "Life is not defined by what you have, even when you have a lot." ~ "People who don't know God and the way he works fuss over these things, but you know both God and how he works. Steep your life in God-reality, God-initiative, God-provi-sions. Don't worry about missing out. You'll find all your everyday human concerns will be met." ~

Honor God with everything you own. Give him the first and the best. ~ Don't be obsessed with getting more material things. Be re-laxed with what you have. God assured us, "I'll never let you down, never walk off and leave you." ~ The world and all its wanting, want-ing, wanting is on the way out—but whoever does what God wants is set for eternity.

დⓞ❧

[Pr. 23:4-5; 1 Tim. 6:10; Mk. 10:23; Mt. 6:19-21; Pr. 11:28; Lk. 12:15; Mt. 6:32-33; Pr. 3:9; Heb. 13:5; 1 Jn. 2:17]

What do your material possessions indicate about you?

TAKING LIFE SERIOUSLY

YOUR LIFE IS A JOURNEY you must travel with a deep cosciousness of God. It cost God plenty to get you out of that dead-end, empty-headed life you grew up in. ~ The empty-headed treat life as a plaything; the perceptive grasp its meaning and make a go of it. ~

Who out there has a lust for life? Can't wait each day to come upon beauty? ~ "Steep your life in God-reality, God-initiative, God-provisions. Don't worry about missing out. You'll find all your every-day human concerns will be met." ~ "Don't set people up as experts over your life, letting them tell you what to do. Save that authority for God. Let *him* tell you what to do." ~

It pays to take life seriously. Things work out when you trust in God. ~ "Give away your life. You'll find life given back, but not mere-ly given back—given back with bonus and blessing. Giving, not get-ting, is the way. Generosity begets generosity." ~

In this way we are like the various parts of a human body. Each part gets its meaning from the body as a whole, not the other way around. The body we're talking about is Christ's body of chosen people. Each of us finds our meaning and function as a part of his body. ~

"Put your mind on your life with God. The way to life—to God!—is vigorous and requires your total attention." ~ "If you grasp and cling to life on your terms, you'll lose it, but if you let that life go, you'll get life on God's terms."

∽◦ ◦∾

[1 Pet. 1:17-18; Pr. 15:21; Ps. 34:12; Mt. 6:33; Mt. 23:9; Pr. 16:20; Lk. 6:38; Rom. 12:4-5; Lk. 13:24; Lk. 17:33]

Sometimes we have a vague sense of longing for something that is missing in our lives, something "more," something that would be meaningful to us. Where do you feel drawn to find meaning in your life?

GETTING YOUR INSIDE WORLD PUT RIGHT

HUMANS ARE SATISFIED with whatever looks good. God probes for what *is* good. ~ God is in charge of human life, watching and examining us inside and out. ~ Keep vigilant watch over your heart. *That's* where life starts. Don't talk out of both sides of your mouth. Avoid careless banter, white lies, and gossip. Keep your eyes straight ahead. Ignore all sideshow distractions. ~

We justify our actions by appearances; God examines our motives. ~ A bad motive can't achieve a good end. Double-talk brings you double trouble. ~ Mixed motives twist life into tangles; pure motives take you straight down the road. ~ The fear of human opinion disables; trusting in God protects you from that. ~

Do everything readily and cheerfully—no bickering, no second-guessing allowed! Go out into the world uncorrupted, a breath of fresh air in this squalid and polluted society. Provide people with a glimpse of good living and of the living God. ~ When the Master comes, he will bring out in the open and place in evidence all kinds of things we never even dreamed of—inner motives and purposes and prayers. ~

Jesus said, "You're blessed when you get your inside world— your mind and heart—put right. Then you can see God in the outside world." ~ "The health of the apple tells the health of the tree. You must begin with your own life-giving lives. It's who you are, not what you say and do, that counts. Your true being brims over into true words and deeds."

∽◎ ◎∾

[Pr. 16:2; Pr. 20:27; Pr. 4:23-25; Pr. 21:2; Pr. 17:20; Pr. 21:8; Pr. 29:25; Phil. 2:14-15; 1 Cor. 4:5; Mt. 5:8; Lk. 6:44-45]

What are some of the more basic reasons why you do the things you do?

WHEN YOU STAY ON COURSE

YOU'RE BLESSED when you stay on course, walking steadily on the road revealed by God. You're blessed when you follow his directions, doing your best to find him. That's right—you don't go off on your own; you walk straight along the road he set. ~ Exercise your freedom by serving God, not by breaking the rules. ~ Merely hearing God's law is a waste of your time if you don't do what he commands. Doing, not hearing, is what makes the difference with God. ~

Jesus said, "Knowing the correct password—saying 'Master, Master,' for instance—isn't going to get you anywhere with me. What is required is serious obedience—*doing* what my Father wills." ~

We know very well that we are not set right with God by rule keeping but only through personal faith in Jesus Christ. How do we know? We tried it—and we had the best system of rules the world has ever seen! Convinced that no human being can please God by self-improvement, we believed in Jesus as the Messiah so that we might be set right before God by trusting in the Messiah, not by trying to be good. . . . If a living relationship with God could come by rule keeping, then Christ died unnecessarily. ~

Here's how we can be sure that we know God in the right way: Keep his commandments. If someone claims, "I know him well!" but doesn't keep his commandments, he's obviously a liar. His life doesn't match his words. But the one who keeps God's word is the person in whom we see God's mature love. This is the only way to be sure we're in God. Anyone who claims to be intimate with God ought to live the same kind of life Jesus lived.

⁓◌ ◌⁓

[Ps. 119:1-3; 1 Pet. 2:16; Rom. 2:13; Mt. 7:21; Gal. 2:16,21; 1 Jn. 2:3-6]

What can you do to make obeying God something positive and not something that seems mechanical and legalistic?

KEEP COMPANY WITH GOD

IF YOU DON'T KNOW what you're doing, pray to the Father. He loves to help. You'll get his help, and won't be condescended to when you ask for it. Ask boldly, believingly, without a second thought. People who "worry their prayers" are like wind-whipped waves. ~ "Don't bargain with God. Be direct. Ask for what you need. This is not a cat-and-mouse, hide-and-seek game we're in." ~

Jesus said, "Find a quiet, secluded place so you won't be tempted to role-play before God. Just be there as simply and honestly as you can manage. The focus will shift from you to God, and you will begin to sense his grace." ~ Keep company with God. Get in on the best. ~

"The world is full of so-called prayer warriors who are prayer-ignorant. They're full of formulas and programs and advice, peddling techniques for getting what you want from God. Don't fall for that nonsense. This is your Father you are dealing with, and he knows better than you what you need. . . .

"In prayer there is a connection between what God does and what you do. You can't get forgiveness from God, for instance, without also forgiving others. If you refuse to do your part, you cut yourself off from God's part." ~

Make this your common practice: Confess your sins to each other and pray for each other so that you can live together whole and healed. The prayer of a person living right with God is something powerful to be reckoned with. ~ Pray all the time. ~ God's there, listening for all who pray—for all who pray and mean it.

∽∞ ∾

[Jas. 1:5-6; Lk. 11:10; Mt. 6:6; Ps. 37:4; Mt. 6:7-8,14-15; Jas. 5:16; 1 Thes. 5:17; Ps. 145:18]

Since prayer is communication with God, describe both sides of your communication with Him.

DISCOVER BEAUTY IN EVERYONE

GET ALONG with each other. Don't be stuck-up. Make friends with nobodies. Don't be the great somebody. . . . Discover beauty in everyone. If you've got it in you, get along with everybody. ~

Jesus said, "Don't pick on people, jump on their failures, criticize their faults—unless, of course, you want the same treatment. Don't condemn those who are down; that hardness can boomerang. Be easy on people; you'll find life a lot easier. Give away your life; you'll find life given back, but not merely given back—given back with bonus and blessing. Giving, not getting, is the way. Generosity begets generosity." ~

Live creatively, friends. If someone falls into sin, forgivingly restore him, saving your critical comments for yourself. *You* might be needing forgiveness before the day's out. Stoop down and reach out to those who are oppressed. Share their burdens, and so complete Christ's law. If you think you are too good for that, you are badly deceived. ~ Regard prisoners as if you were in prison with them. Look on victims of abuse as if what happened to them had happened to you. ~

"Here is a simple rule of thumb for behavior: Ask yourself what you want people to do for you; then grab the initiative and do it for *them*! If you only love the lovable, do you expect a pat on the back? Run-of-the-mill sinners do that." ~

The old life is gone; a new life burgeons! Look at it! All this comes from the God who settled the relationship between us and him, and then called us to settle our relationships with each other. ~ God's gift has restored our relationship with him and given us back our lives. And there's more life to come—an eternity of life!

৩ ৩৩

[Rom. 12:16-18; Lk. 6:37-38; Gal. 6:1-3; Heb. 13:3; Lk. 6:31-32; 2 Cor. 5:17-18; Titus 3:7]

How does God want you to relate to other people—and to him?

WHEN A BASIC HOLINESS PERMEATES THINGS

JESUS SAID, "Are you tired? Worn out? Burned out on religion? Come to me. Get away with me and you'll recover your life. I'll show you how to take a real rest." ~ "Come off by yourselves. Let's take a break and get a little rest." ~ "Here's what I want you to do: Find a quiet, secluded place so you won't be tempted to role-play before God. Just be there as simply and honestly as you can manage. The focus will shift from you to God, and you will begin to sense his grace." ~ "In this godless world you will continue to experience difficulties. But take heart! I've conquered the world." ~

Be cheerful. Keep things in good repair. Keep your spirits up. Think in harmony. Be agreeable. Do all that, and the God of love and peace will be with you for sure. ~ "You're blessed when you can show people how to cooperate instead of compete or fight. That's when you discover who you really are, and your place in God's family." ~

What happens when we live God's way? He brings gifts into our lives, much the same way that fruit appears in an orchard—things like affection for others, exuberance about life, serenity. We develop a willingness to stick with things, a sense of compassion in the heart, and a conviction that a basic holiness permeates things and people. We find ourselves involved in loyal commitments. ~

Let the peace of Christ keep you in tune with each other, in step with each other. None of this going off and doing your own thing. And cultivate thankfulness. ~ Relax, everything's going to be all right. Rest, everything's coming together. Open your hearts, love is on the way!

∽◉ ◉∾

[Mt. 11:28; Mk. 6:31; Mt. 6:6; Jn. 16:33; 2 Cor. 13:11; Mt. 5:9; Gal. 5:22; Col. 3:15; Jude 2]

How can you maintain a state of rest when the whole world around you is pulsating with chaos?

TO SEE WHAT YOUR EYES CAN'T SEE

DON'T TRY TO FIGURE OUT everything on your own. Listen for God's voice in everything you do, everywhere you go. He's the one who will keep you on track. Don't assume that you know it all. Run to God! Run from evil! ~ Open up before God. Keep nothing back. He'll do whatever needs to be done. ~

Jesus said, "Don't look for shortcuts to God. The market is flooded with surefire, easygoing formulas for a successful life that can be practiced in your spare time. Don't fall for that stuff." ~ "If your first concern is to look after yourself, you'll never find yourself. But if you forget about yourself and look to me, you'll find both yourself and me." ~ This world is not your home, so don't make yourselves cozy in it. Don't indulge your ego at the expense of your soul. ~

"Use your head—and heart!—to discern what is right, to test what is authentically right." ~ People try to put a shroud over truth. But the basic reality of God is plain enough. Open your eyes and there it is! By taking a long and thoughtful look at what God has created, people have always been able to see what their eyes as such can't see: eternal power, for instance, and the mystery of his divine being. So nobody has a good excuse. ~

It's impossible to please God apart from faith. And why? Because anyone who wants to approach God must believe both that he exists *and* that he cares enough to respond to those who seek him. ~ "Then you will experience for yourselves the truth, and the truth will free you."

꼬ꙮ꼬

[Pr. 3:5-7; Ps. 37:5; Mt. 7:13; Mt. 10:39; 1 Pet. 2:11; Jn. 7:24; Rom. 1:18-20; Heb. 11:6; Jn. 8:32]

While we are going through our ongoing journey of seeking God, he is also seeking us. How can this double seeking become "finding"?

LIVE OUT YOUR GOD-CREATED IDENTITY

MAKE A CAREFUL EXPLORATION of who you are and the work you have been given, and then sink yourself into that. Don't be impressed with yourself. Don't compare yourself with others. Each of you must take responsibility for doing the creative best you can with your own life. ~ What matters is not your outer appearance—the styling of your hair, the jewelry you wear, the cut of your clothes—but your inner disposition. Cultivate inner beauty, the gentle, gracious kind that God delights in. ~

"Live out your God-created identity. Live generously and graciously toward others, the way God lives toward you." ~ "If you walk around with your nose in the air, you're going to end up flat on your face. But if you're content to be simply yourself, you will become more than yourself." ~

Obsession with self is a dead end; attention to God leads us out into the open, into a spacious, free life. Focusing on the self is the opposite of focusing on God. Anyone completely absorbed in self ignores God, ends up thinking more about self than God. That person ignores who God is and what he is doing. And God isn't pleased at being ignored. ~

It's in Christ that we find out who we are and what we are living for. Long before we first heard of Christ and got our hopes up, he had his eye on us, had designs on us for glorious living, part of the overall purpose he is working out in everything and everyone. ~ Don't you see that you can't live however you please, squandering what God paid such a high price for? The physical part of you is not some piece of property belonging to the spiritual part of you. God owns the whole works.

෴

[Gal. 6:4-5; 1 Pet. 3:3-4; Mt. 5:48; Lk. 14:11; Rom. 8:6-8; Eph. 1:11; 1 Cor. 6:19-20]

Who are you? What do you think of yourself?

STRENGTH IS FOR SERVICE

OUR LORD IS GREAT, with limitless strength. We'll never comprehend what he knows and does. ~ Human wisdom is so tinny, so impotent, next to the seeming absurdity of God. Human strength can't begin to compete with God's "weakness." ~

I was given the gift of a handicap to keep me in constant touch with my limitations. Satan's angel did his best to get me down. What he in fact did was push me to my knees. No danger then of walking around high and mighty! At first I didn't think of it as a gift, and begged God to remove it. Three times I did that, and then he told me, "My grace is enough; it's all you need. My strength comes into its own in your weakness."

Once I heard that, I was glad to let it happen. I quit focusing on the handicap and began appreciating the gift. It was a case of Christ's strength moving in on my weakness. Now I take limitations in stride, and with good cheer, these limitations that cut me down to size—abuse, accidents, opposition, bad breaks. I just let Christ take over! And so the weaker I get, the stronger I become. ~ Less is more and more is less. ~

Those of us who are strong and able in the faith need to step in and lend a hand to those who falter, and not just do what is most convenient for us. Strength is for service, not status. ~ It is strength that endures the unendurable and spills over into joy, thanking the Father who makes us strong enough to take part in everything bright and beautiful that he has for us. ~

Jesus said, "I am the Vine, you are the branches. When you're joined with me and I with you, the relation intimate and organic, the harvest is sure to be abundant. Separated, you can't produce a thing."

∽◉◍

[Ps. 147:5; 1 Cor. 1:25; 2 Cor. 12:7-10; Ps. 37:16; Rom. 15:1; Col. 1:11-12; Jn. 15:5]

List your personal strengths and describe how God wants each strength to be applied to other people and to him.

LEARNING THE UNFORCED RHYTHMS OF GRACE

I'M AWAKE ALL NIGHT—not a wink of sleep. I can't even say what's bothering me. I go over the days one by one, I ponder the years gone by. ~ God, you've kept track of my every toss and turn through the sleepless nights, each tear entered in your ledger, each ache written in your book. ~

Jesus said, "Walk with me and work with me—watch how I do it. Learn the unforced rhythms of grace. I won't lay anything heavy or ill-fitting on you. Keep company with me and you'll learn to live freely and lightly." ~ "I'm leaving you well and whole. That's my parting gift to you. Peace. I don't leave you the way you're used to being left—feeling abandoned, bereft. So don't be upset." ~

Worry weighs us down; a cheerful word picks us up. ~ Don't fret or worry. Instead of worrying, pray. Let petitions and praises shape your worries into prayers, letting God know your concerns. Before you know it, a sense of God's wholeness, everything coming together for good, will come and settle you down. It's wonderful what happens when Christ displaces worry at the center of your life. ~

Pile your troubles on God's shoulders—he'll carry your load, he'll help you out. ~ People who won't settle down, wandering hither and yon, are like restless birds flitting to and fro. ~ Don't burn out. Keep yourselves fueled and aflame. Be alert servants of the Master. ~ Let's not allow ourselves to get fatigued doing good. At the right time we will harvest a good crop if we don't give up, or quit. ~ For God is greater than our worried hearts and knows more about us than we do ourselves.

ᴄᴏ ᴏᴡ

[Ps. 77:4-5; Ps. 56:8; Mt. 11:29-30; Jn. 14:27; Pr. 12:25; Phil. 4:6-7; Ps. 55:22; Pr. 27:8; Rom. 12:11; Gal. 6:9; 1 Jn. 3:20]

Before you can "Pile your troubles on God's shoulders," you probably need to take an inventory of just what those troubles or stress points are. So, what are they?

DISTRESS THAT DRIVES US TO GOD

I CAN SEE NOW, God, that your decisions are right. Your testing has taught me what's true and right. ~ My troubles turned out all for the best—they forced me to learn from your textbook. ~

We know how troubles can develop passionate patience in us, and how that patience in turn forges the tempered steel of virtue, keeping us alert for whatever God will do next. ~ Distress that drives us to God does that. It turns us around. It gets us back in the way of salvation. We never regret that kind of pain. But those who let distress drive them away from God are full of regrets, end up on a deathbed of regrets. ~ Pure gold put in the fire comes out of it *proved* pure; genuine faith put through this suffering comes out *proved* genuine. ~ Better to be confronted by the Master now than to face a fiery confrontation later. ~

There's far more to this life than trusting in Christ. There's also suffering for him. And the suffering is as much a gift as the trusting. ~ Anyone who wants to live all out for Christ is in for a lot of trouble; there's no getting around it. ~ Think of your sufferings as a weaning from that old sinful habit of always expecting to get your own way. Then you'll be able to live out your days free to pursue what God wants instead of being tyrannized by what you want. ~

Consider it a sheer gift, friends, when tests and challenges come at you from all sides. You know that under pressure, your faith-life is forced into the open and shows its true colors. So don't try to get out of anything prematurely. Let it do its work so you become mature and well-developed, not deficient in any way.

෴

[Ps. 119:75; Ps. 119:71; Rom. 5:3-4; 2 Cor. 7:10; 1 Pet. 1:7; 1 Cor. 11:32; Phil. 1:29; 2 Tim. 3:12; 1 Pet. 4:1-2; Jas. 1:2-4]

In what ways have you grown through suffering?

YOU WANT YOUR OWN WAY

"STAY ALERT. Be in prayer so you don't wander into temptation without even knowing you're in danger. There is a part of you that is eager, ready for anything in God. But there's another part that's as lazy as an old dog sleeping by the fire." ~ Don't be so naive and self-confident. You're not exempt. You could fall flat on your face as easily as anyone else. ~

Don't allow love to turn into lust, setting off a downhill slide into sexual promiscuity, filthy practices, or bullying greed. ~ Where do you think all these appalling wars and quarrels come from? Do you think they just happen? Think again. They come about because you want your own way, and fight for it deep inside yourselves. You lust for what you don't have and are willing to kill to get it. ~

Don't let anyone under pressure to give in to evil say, "God is trying to trip me up." God is impervious to evil, and puts evil in no one's way. The temptation to give in to evil comes from us and only us. We have no one to blame but the leering, seducing flare-up of our own lust. Lust gets pregnant, and has a baby: sin! Sin grows up to adulthood, and becomes a real killer. ~

Since we do not have the excuse of ignorance, everything—and I do mean everything—connected with that old way of life has to go. It's rotten through and through. Get rid of it! And then take on an entirely new way of life—a God-fashioned life, a life renewed from the inside and working itself into your conduct as God accurately reproduces his character in you. ~

No test or temptation that comes your way is beyond the course of what others have had to face. All you need to remember is that God will never let you down. He'll never let you be pushed past your limit. He'll always be there to help you come through it.

✌ ฿

[Mt. 26:41; 1 Cor. 10:12; Eph. 5:3; Jas. 4:1-2; Jas. 1:13-15; Eph. 4:22; 1 Cor. 10:13]

DAY 29

What are your most serious temptations and how can you deal positively with them?

GOD ALONE KNOWS IT ALL

IT'S BETTER TO BE WISE than strong. Intelligence outranks muscle any day. ~ Knowing what is right is like deep water in the heart; a wise person draws from the well within. ~ Wise men and women are always learning, always listening for fresh insights. ~

Become wise by walking with the wise; hang out with fools and watch your life fall to pieces. ~ Do you want to be counted wise, to build a reputation for wisdom? Here's what you do: Live well, live wisely, live humbly. It's the way you live, not the way you talk, that counts. Mean-spirited ambition isn't wisdom. Boasting that you are wise isn't wisdom. Twisting the truth to make yourselves sound wise isn't wisdom. It's the furthest thing from wisdom—it's animal cunning, devilish conniving. Whenever you're trying to look better than others or get the better of others, things fall apart and everyone ends up at the others' throats.

Real wisdom, God's wisdom, begins with a holy life and is characterized by getting along with others. It is gentle and reasonable, overflowing with mercy and blessings, not hot one day and cold the next, not two-faced. You can develop a healthy, robust community that lives right with God and enjoy its results *only* if you do the hard work of getting along with each other, treating each other with dignity and honor. ~

Don't fool yourself. Don't think that you can be wise merely by being up-to-date with the times. ~ If you think you know it all, you're a fool for sure; real survivors learn wisdom from others. ~ Human wisdom is so tinny, so impotent, next to the seeming absurdity of God. ~ We never really know enough until we recognize that God alone knows it all.

౨౦ ౦౨

[Pr. 24:5; Pr. 20:5; 18:15; Pr. 13:20; Jas. 3:13-18; 1 Cor. 3:18; Pr. 28:26; 1 Cor. 1:25; 1 Cor. 8:3]

How can you on an ongoing basis develop greater wisdom?

No Waste of Time or Effort

IF GOD DOESN'T BUILD the house, the builders only build shacks. ~ God cares about honesty in the workplace. Your business is his business. ~ Don't hold back. Throw yourselves into the work of the Master, confident that nothing you do for him is a waste of time or effort. ~

You call out to God for help and he helps—he's a good Father that way. But don't forget, he's also a responsible Father, and won't let you get by with sloppy living. Your life is a journey you must travel with a deep consciousness of God. ~ As you learn more and more how God works, you will learn how to do *your* work. We pray that you'll have the strength to stick it out over the long haul—not the grim strength of gritting your teeth but the glory-strength God gives. It is strength that endures the unendurable. ~

Well-done work has its own reward. ~ Observe people who are good at their work—skilled workers are always in demand and admired. ~ The diligent find freedom in their work; the lazy are oppressed by work. ~

Get along among yourselves, each of you doing your part. Our counsel is that you warn the freeloaders to get a move on. Gently encourage the stragglers, and reach out for the exhausted, pulling them to their feet. Be patient with each person, attentive to individual needs. ~ Get an honest job so that you can help others who can't work. ~ Don't burn out. Keep yourselves fueled and aflame. Be alert servants of the Master. ~

As long as I'm alive in this body, there is good work for me to do.

[Ps. 127:1; Pr. 16:11; 1 Cor. 15:58; 1 Pet. 1:17; Col. 1:10-11; Pr. 12:14; Pr. 22:29; Pr. 12:24; 1 Thes. 5:13-14; Eph. 4:28; Rom. 12:11; Phil. 1:22]

What are the best ways to make work meaningful and to keep it from becoming drudgery?